The Reluctant Tales of Titch and Tup and The Triple Troubles

David Gooch

First published in 2025 by Blossom Spring Publishing
The Reluctant Tales of Titch and Tup and The Triple Troubles
Copyright © 2025 David Gooch
ISBN 978-1-917938-19-8
E: admin@blossomspringpublishing.com
W: www.blossomspringpublishing.com
All rights reserved under International Copyright Law.
Contents and/or cover may not be reproduced in whole
or in part without the express written consent
of the publisher.
Names, characters, places and incidents
are either products of the author's imagination
or are used fictitiously.

"I can't believe you have opened this book after being warned not to. Do you do anything you are told?"

"Blooming Kids"

"If we can find somewhere to hide Titch, then there is no story. And the kids will get bored and leave."

"Great idea Tup. Let's see what we can find."

"Over there Titch. That looks perfect."

"Brilliant hiding place, Tup."

"I bet those kids haven't a clue where we are."

"Thank you, Kids! With your help we have caught Titch."

Haha! Haha!

Haha

"We will take him away and make him fill our paddling pool."

Haha!

"Oh forget it! What do kids know anyway?

I'll think of something myself."

"Come on Titch, hurry up and fill our paddling Pool. It's hot and we need to cool down."

"Poor Titch. How can I help him?"

"I know, I'll phone Bionic Bob.

I'm sure he will help me rescue Titch from the Triple Troubles."

"Hello Bionic Bob. I need you now! The Triple Troubles have caught Titch, and we must help him escape."

"So sorry Tup. But I can't help. Last time I met The Triple Troubles they hid my bionic leg for two days!

I could only hop everywhere. Good luck. Bye."

Oh! There goes Happy Hannah. I wonder if she would help me rescue Titch. "Hello Happy Hannah."

"Hello Tup."
"It's a lovely day for a walk."
"Yes it is. I'm very happy Today."

"I'm so pleased to see you Happy Hannah. The Triple Troubles are being horrid to Titch."

"Oh dear!"

"Oh dear!"

"Oh dear!"

"Together, we may be able to rescue him. Please help me?"

"Oh dear! Last time I met the Triple Troubles, I was unhappy for a week. So sorry Tup.

But I have just remembered something very important to do. Byeee!"

"This is lovely. If we can catch some of the readers, they could mow the grass and make us sandwiches and drinks. That would then be a perfect day!"

"Poor Titch."

That's lucky, it's Speedy Steve. "Hiya! Please stop for a moment to chat. Titch needs help with The Triple Troubles. They are up to their horrid ways again."

"The Triple Troubles! That's not good. Let me think about it for a minute."

"Wait Speedy Steve. Please wait! It's only a little help Titch needs. Don't go!"

"I'm not scared of The Triple Troubles Tup, and I would help. But I'm feeling extra speedy today. So, I don't really have the time. See you later."

"After the count of three, call out 'Hello' as loud as you can. It may frighten The Triple Troubles and give Titch a chance to escape.

Ready?

1, 2, 3

Hello!"

"I said **Loud!** That was rubbish! What is the matter with you kids? Forgotten how to shout, have we?

Try again!"

"Wow, Tup! That was great. What a brilliant idea. How did you make so much noise by yourself?"

"I'm just clever I guess."

"We all know you are not that clever Tup. Come on, tell the truth. How did you do it?"

"Alright, alright. I have told Titch the truth that you kids helped me rescue him from the Triple Troubles.

But just remember that I came up with the idea. And that makes me very clever indeed."

"We realise that we should thank you kids for helping to rescue Titch.
So, erm, thank you!
What? You can't hear it? Oh, sorry!

Thank you!

Be warned though, next time we will hide away somewhere very, very scary. Goodbye."

About the author

Art has consistently been an important part of David's life. Throughout various periods, he has endeavoured to write children's stories with the aspiration that a publisher might consider them. "The Reluctant Tales of Titch and Tup and The Triple Troubles" was conceived in the early 1990s, complete with preliminary illustrations and text. However, due to family responsibilities and work commitments, they were buried away in the 'to-do in the future' ever-growing list.

Recently, with more available time, he decided to work on turning those early ideas into a published children's book. However, adapting to the modern internet requirements of publishers, which do not accept hard copies, proved to be a considerable challenge.

Fortunately, Blossom Spring Publishing liked the story enough, despite his basic IT presentation. And with their encouragement and significant assistance, he has now achieved his goal of publishing a children's book.

www.blossomspringpublishing.com